About the Author

Katrina Liu is an American-born Chinese mom and indie author living in San Francisco, California. Her daughters inspired her to create books where they can see themselves reflected in the characters. She hopes to add more Asian representation into the world of children's books. Katrina has written and published several titles that feature Asian-American characters and culture. She also has many bilingual books available in Chinese and English for non-native speakers.

For more books by Katrina Liu visit
www.lycheepress.com

ISBN 978-1-953281-62-3

Copyright © 2022 by Katrina Liu. All rights reserved. No part of this book may be reproduced, transmitted, or stored in an information retrieval system in any form or by any means, graphic, electronic, or mechanical, including photocopying, taping, and recording, without prior written permission from the publisher. First edition 2022. Also available in a bilingual Chinese editions.

For Mina & Leah,

The inspiration for everything I do.

Mama just told me something really exciting. She says there's a baby in her belly. I'm going to be a big sister!

Mama says that's because Baby is still tiny, only about the size of a blueberry, but growing every day.

Mama says Baby is now the size of a strawberry. I giggle. I wonder why she keeps referring to Baby as fruit? A baby isn't food! But it's okay. I love fruit!

Today we're making lemonade! Mama says Baby is the size of a lemon now. But lemons are sour! I hope Baby is sweet.

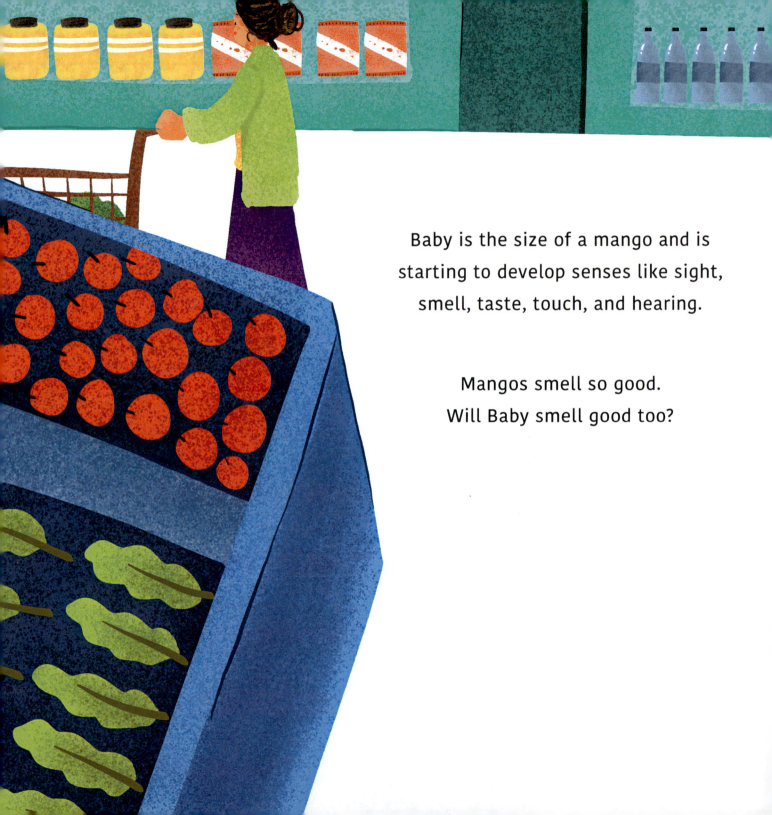

Baby is the size of a mango and is starting to develop senses like sight, smell, taste, touch, and hearing.

Mangos smell so good.
Will Baby smell good too?

Baby can hear us now.
So I sing my favorite song for Baby!

Baby is now as big as a coconut! Mama says Baby also has eyelashes and eyebrows.

Coconuts are hairy. I wonder if Baby will come out hairy too?

Mama's belly is getting bigger. She says Baby is the size of a pineapple and a really good kicker.

I feel Mama's belly. Oof!
That's one strong baby.

Maybe Baby will want to learn kung fu!

Baby is now as big as a cantaloupe!
It's getting harder to sit on Mama's lap, so
I turn around to give Baby a big hug instead!

Mama tells me I'm going to be the best big sister.

Baby is as big as a watermelon.
Mama says it's almost time.

I can't wait to read my favorite stories to Baby!

Today is the day! Baby is here!
I love my baby sister so much.
She's sweeter than any fruit I've ever had!

Made in United States
North Haven, CT
23 March 2023

34449350R00015